The
United States:
A Christian Nation

By David Josiah Brewer

Foreword and Afterword by
Martin Mawyer

D1603751

PRB PUBLISHING

THE UNITED STATES: A CHRISTIAN NATION

BY DAVID J. BREWER

Originally published in 1905 by The John C. Winston Company,
Philadelphia, Pa., as a series of three lectures to the students
of Haverford College, Haverford, Pa., presented by
David J. Brewer, Associate Justice of the Supreme Court of the United States.

Reprinted in 2016 by PRB Publishing

Foreword and Afterword by Martin Mawyer

ISBN-13:
9780692752609

Managing Editor: Patti A. Pierucci

Consulting Editor: Alec Rooney

Printed in the United States of America

Cover Art:
Painting on board by Kristina Elaine Greer
Cover Design by The Kirchman Studio

Foreword

I n 1892, Supreme Court Associate Justice David Josiah Brewer made history when he ruled from the highest court that the United States "is a Christian Nation." When the ruling was issued, there were no opposing editorials, street brawls or longwinded outcries from universities, historians or disgruntled politicians.

At the time, no one seemed to notice or care. The statement was no more controversial or upsetting than saying America was a republic. It was obvious. What was there to argue about?

In all his writings, interviews and speeches, Justice Brewer never explained why he felt it necessary to declare America a Christian nation. Perhaps he was simply reacting to comments made a decade earlier by German philosopher Friedrich Nietzsche, who famously said that "God is dead."

At the time, Nietzsche's "God is dead" theory was gaining popularity among the European elite as a way of dispensing with the spiritual nature of Christianity while keeping its values, ethics and morals. Certainly, Nietzsche was a primary cause of Europe entering into a post-Christian world—a world where Jesus is loved, admired and emulated, but where his spiritual teachings are sacrificed on the cross.

If Brewer had personal reasons for declaring America a Christian nation, they are now lost in history. But for many years after (even up until his death in 1920), Justice Brewer would often refer to his "Christian Nation" ruling during public appearances before agreeable audiences. Today it has become the hallmark of his legacy.

The case itself was only mildly remarkable.

At issue was an 1880 law that prohibited the importation or migration of foreign workers to perform labor in the United States (*Holy Trinity v. United States*).

Seven years after the law's passage, the Church of the Holy Trinity in New York City hired E. Walpole Warren from England to be its pastor and rector. The church was subsequently charged with violating the statute by bringing in a foreign worker, and convicted. An appellate court upheld the conviction.

But in 1892 the U.S. Supreme Court overturned the ruling, saying the law could not be applied to ministers or to those in professional oc-cupations (those who use their brains, rather than muscles, to work). After all, Justice Brewer wrote for the unanimous court, " ... this is a Christian nation."

Throughout his career, Brewer's Christian beliefs would temper many of his rulings, speeches and actions.

His biographer, Michael Brodhead, said, "Indeed, his responses to the public questions of the day were to a great extent shaped by the Christian beliefs of this son of a missionary."

Supreme Court Associate Justice David Josiah Brewer, who ruled in 1892 that America "is a Christian nation."

David Brewer was born in Smyrna, Turkey, to missionary par-ents on June 20, 1837. His father, the Rev. Josiah Brewer, was a Yale grad-uate who traveled to Turkey for the purpose of converting Jews to Christianity. A cholera epidemic and a lack of financial support forced the Brewers to return to Wethersfield, Conn., in 1838.

Over the next 15 years the elder Brewer would travel from town to dusty town, as well as to larger cities, advocating Christ, prison re-form and the end of slavery. His son, David, quickly adopted his fa-ther's passion for all these causes and included some of his own, such as women's suffrage and an enhanced role for women in all professions.

Since he took such liberal positions on the issues of his day, it is surprising that some contemporary writers describe Justice Brewer as an "ultra-conservative."

As a judge in Kansas, Justice Brewer supported the rights of women to hold property in their own names. He upheld their right to serve as school supervisors. In 1905, he even gave a speech at Vassar College endorsing the idea of a female president of the United States, which was revolutionary for the time.

In addition, he authored one of the first judicial opinions upholding the right of African-American citizens to vote in a general election.

Justice Brewer was far from an ultra-conservative, but it was probably correct to describe him, as author Andy Schmookler wrote in the Daily Kos, as "one of the most unabashedly religious justices to ever serve."

Brewer once stated, "I glory in the fact that my father was an old-line abolitionist, and one thing which he instilled into my youthful soul was the conviction that liberty, personal and political, is the God-given right of every individual, and I expect to live and die in that faith."

Like his father, Brewer graduated from Yale. He received his law degree from Albany Law School in the spring of 1858.

In the same year he would depart for Kansas, where he briefly practiced law. Young and ambitious, he wouldn't stay long in the Sunflower State. He quickly opted to head west in search of gold at Pike's Peak in Colorado. When that venture failed, he headed back east to live with his parents in Stockbridge, Mass.

After a short stay, Brewer became restless again and decided to return to Kansas. He landed in the small town of Leavenworth, which had a population of just 10,000.

For a couple of years he was employed as an unassuming notary public, but his fortunes would soon turn. He found a job with a law firm, and was appointed as commissioner of the Federal Circuit Court in 1861. From there his career would skyrocket.

He was elected judge of the county probate court, and in 1865 was elected judge of the first judicial district court of Kansas.

Eventually he would be elected to three six-year terms on the Kansas Supreme Court. In 1884 President Chester Alan Arthur, America's 21st president, appointed him to the Eighth Circuit Appeals Court.

Five years later, after the resignation of Supreme Court Justice Stanley Matthews due to a sudden illness, President Benjamin Harrison nominated Brewer to the Supreme Court.

After 20 years on the High Court, Justice Brewer had gained a reputation for limiting the power of government.

He rejected what today is called the "nanny state," and advocated a narrow interpretation of police power.

Writing for the Supreme Court in *Budd v. New York* (1892), Justice Brewer said:

"The paternal theory of government is to me odious. The utmost possible liberty to the individual, and the fullest possible protection for him and his property, is both the limitation and the duty of government."

Highlighting the difference between America and the Old World, Brewer said that in times past "the individual lived for the nation. But here, the nation exists for the individual."

A member of the First Congregational Church, Brewer believed strongly that the character of America was a reflection of its people.

"You cannot disassociate the character of the nation and that of its citizens," Brewer said during a lecture at Yale on "American Citizenship."

In a series of speeches, Brewer would encourage all citizens to fulfill their duty by contributing their skills, talents, wisdom, knowledge and actions to making America a better nation.

"We are not only born into families but also into citizenship in a nation," Brewer said. "Of all the obligations of citizen to nation none is greater than our obligation as citizens to the Republic. The responsibilities of citizenship are nowhere more sacred and solemn."

Justice Brewer died in 1910, though historical records conflict on the manner of his death. Some claim a heart attack took his life, others an aneurysm. All seem to agree he died in bed waiting for a doctor to arrive. He is buried in a cemetery in Leavenworth, a town that has also named an elementary school after him.

Sadly, his large tombstone bears no remarkable words of wisdom, nor any tribute or reminder that he was the first Supreme Court justice to call America "A Christian Nation."

Martin Mawyer
President, Founder
Christian Action Network
Lynchburg, Virginia

May 2016

From the provisions of the donor to Haverford College:

"The money ($10,000) to be kept safely invested, the Income only to be used for an annual course or series of lectures before the senior class of the College and other students, on the Bible, its history, and its literature, and, as way may open for it, upon its doctrine and its teaching."

Contents

THREE LECTURES

PART 1: THE UNITED STATES: A CHRISTIAN NATION

Chapter 1: Christianity in our State Charters   8

Chapter 2: Sundays Excepted   19

PART 2: OUR DUTY AS CITIZENS

Chapter 3: Christianity and Patriotism   30

Chapter 4: Give Honor Where Due   33

Chapter 5: A Positive Influence   39

PART 3: THE PROMISE AND THE POSSIBILITIES OF THE FUTURE

Chapter 6: The Great Melting Pot   49

Chapter 7: Building a Better Mankind   55

Part 1:

The United States:
A Christian Nation

CHAPTER 1:

Christianity in our State Charters

We classify nations in various ways. As, for instance, by their form of government. One is a kingdom, another an empire, and still another a republic. Also by race. Great Britain is an Anglo-Saxon nation, France a Gallic, Germany a Teutonic, Russia a Slav. And still again by religion. One is a Mohammedan (Islamic) nation, others are heathen, and still others are Christian nations.

This republic is classified among the Christian nations of the world. It was so formally declared by the Supreme Court of the United States. In the case of Holy Trinity Church vs. United States, 143 U.S. 71, that court, after mentioning various circumstances, added, "these and many other matters which might be noticed, add a volume of unofficial declarations to the mass of organic utterances that this is a Christian nation."

But in what sense can it be called a Christian nation? Not in the sense that Christianity is the established religion or that the people are in any manner compelled to support it. On the contrary, the Constitution specifically provides that "Congress shall make no law respecting an establishment of religion, or prohibiting the free exercise thereof." Neither is it Christian in the sense that all its citizens are either in fact or name Christians.

On the contrary, all religions have free scope within our borders. Numbers of our people profess other religions, "and many reject all. Nor is it Christian in the sense that a profession of Christianity is a condition of holding office or otherwise engaging in the public service, or essential to recognition either politically or socially. In fact the government as a legal organization is independent of all religions.

Nevertheless, we constantly speak of this republic as a Christian nation, in fact, as the leading Christian nation of the world. This popular use of the term certainly has significance. It is not a mere creation of the imagination. It is not a term of derision but has a substantial basis, one which justifies its use. Let us analyze a little and see what is the basis.

Its use has had from the early settlements on our shores and still has an official foundation. It is only about three centuries since the beginnings of civilized life within the limits of these United States. And those beginnings were in a marked and marvelous degree identified with Christianity. The commission from Ferdinand and Isabella to Columbus recites that "it is hoped that by God's assistance some of the continents and islands in the ocean will be discovered." The first colonial grant, that made to Sir Walter Raleigh, in 1584, authorized him to enact statutes for the government of the proposed colony, provided that "they be not against the true Christian faith now professed in the

> *"Nevertheless, every sector denomination of people ought to observe the Sabbath, or the Lord's Day, and keep up and support some sort of religious worship, which to them shall seem most agreeable to the revealed will of God."*
>
> From the Constitution of Vermont, 1777, granting the free exercise of religious worship

Church of England."

The first charter of Virginia, granted by King James I, in 1606, after reciting the application of certain parties for a charter, commenced the grant in these words: "We, greatly commending, and graciously accepting of, their desires for the furtherance of so noble a work, which may, by the providence of Almighty God, hereafter tend to the glory of His Divine Majesty, in propagating the Christian religion to such people as yet live in darkness and miserable ignorance of the true knowledge and worship of God."

And language of similar import is found in subsequent charters of the same colony, from the same king, in 1609 and 1611. The celebrated compact made by the Pilgrims on the Mayflower, in 1620, recites: "Having undertaken for the glory of God and advancement of the Christian faith and the honor of our king and country a voyage to plant the first colony in the northern parts of Virginia."

William Penn, speaking about the role of government in 1682, commented that "the highest attainments (citizens) may arrive at (is) the coming of the blessed second Adam, the Lord from heaven."

The charter of New England, granted by James I, in 1620, after referring to a petition, declares: "We, according to our princely inclination, favoring much their worthy disposition, in hope thereby to advance the enlargement of Christian religion, to the glory of God Almighty."

The charter of Massachusetts Bay, granted in 1629 by Charles I, after several provisions, recites: "Whereby our said people, inhabitants there, may be so religiously, peaceably and civilly governed as their good life and orderly conversation may win and incite the natives of the country to their knowledge and obedience of the only true God and Savior of mankind, and the Christian faith, which in our royal intention and the adventurers free profession, is the principal end of this plantation," which declaration was substantially repeated in the charter of Massachusetts Bay granted by William and Mary, in 1691.

The fundamental orders of Connecticut, under which a provisional government was instituted in 1638-1639, provided: "Forasmuch as it has pleased the Almighty God by the wise disposition of His divine providence so to order and dispose of things that we, the inhabitants and residents of Windsor, Hartford and Wethersfield, are now cohabitating and dwelling in and upon the River of Connecticut and the lands thereto adjoining; and well knowing where a people are gathered together the word of God requires that to maintain the peace and union of such a people there should be an orderly and decent government established according to God, to order and dispose of the affairs of the people at all seasons as occasion shall require; do therefore associate and conjoin ourselves to be as one public state or commonwealth: and do for ourselves and our successors and such as shall be adjoined to us at any time hereafter enter into combination and confederation together to maintain and preserve the liberty and purity of the gospel of our Lord

Jesus which we now profess, as also the discipline of the churches, which, according to the truth of the said gospel, is now practiced amongst us."

In the preamble of the Constitution of 1776 it was declared, "the free fruition of such liberties and privileges as humanity, civility and Christianity call for, as is due to every man in his place and proportion, without impeachment and infringement, hath ever been, and will be the tranquility and stability of churches and commonwealths; and the denial thereof, the disturbance, if not the ruin of both."

In 1638 the first settlers in Rhode Island organized a local government by signing the following agreement:

"We whose names are underwritten do here solemnly in the presence of Jehovah incorporate ourselves into a Body Politick and as He shall help, will submit our persons, lives and estates unto our Lord Jesus Christ, the King of Kings and Lord of Lords, and to all those perfect and most absolute laws of His given us in His holy word of truth, to be guided and judged thereby. Exod. 24: 3, 4; II Chron. 11: 3; II Kings 11:17."

The charter granted to Rhode Island in 1663 naming the petitioners speaks of them as "pursuing, with peaceable and loyal minds, their sober, serious and religious intentions, of godly edifying themselves and one another in the holy Christian faith and worship as they were persuaded; together with the gaining over and conversion of the poor, ignorant Indian natives, in these parts of America, to the sincere profession and obedience of the same faith and worship."

A Zeal for the Christian Faith

The charter of Carolina, granted in 1663 by Charles II, recites that the petitioners [were] "excited with a laudable and pious zeal for the propagation of the Christian faith." In the preface of the frame of government prepared in 1682 by William Penn for Pennsylvania it is said: "They weakly err, that think there is no other use of government than correction, which is the coarsest part of it; daily experience tells us that the care and regulation of many other affairs, more soft, and daily necessary, make up much of the greatest part of government; and which must have followed the peopling of the world, had Adam never fell, and will continue among men, on earth, under the highest attainments they may arrive at, by the coming of the blessed second Adam, the Lord from heaven."

And with the laws prepared to go with the frame of government, it was further provided "that according to the good example of the primitive Christians, and the ease of the creation, every first day of the week, called the Lord's Day, people shall abstain from their common daily labor that they may the better dispose themselves to worship God according to their understandings."

In the charter of privileges granted in 1701 by William Penn to the province of Pennsylvania and territories thereunto belonging (such territories afterwards constituting the State of Delaware), it is recited: "Because no people can be truly happy, though under the greatest enjoyment of civil liberties, if abridged of the freedom of their consciences as to their religious profession and worship; and Almighty God being the only Lord of Conscience, Father of Lights and Spirits, and the author as well as object of all divine knowledge, faith and worship, who only doth enlighten the minds and persuade and convince the understandings of the people, I do hereby grant and declare."

Support for the Lord's Day

The Constitution of Vermont, of 1777, granting the free exercise of religious worship, added, "Nevertheless, every sector denomination of people ought to observe the Sabbath, or the Lord's Day, and keep up and support some sort of religious worship, which to them shall seem most agreeable to the revealed will of God." And this was repeated in the Constitution of 1786.

In the Constitution of South Carolina, of 1778, it was declared that "the Christian Protestant religion shall be deemed and is hereby constituted and declared to be the established religion of this State." And further, that no agreement or union of men upon pretense of religion should be entitled to become incorporated and regarded as a church of the established religion of the State, without agreeing and subscribing to a book of five articles, the third and fourth of which were "that the Christian religion is the true religion; that the holy scriptures of the Old and New Testament are of divine inspiration, and are the rule of faith and practice."

Passing beyond these declarations which are found in the organic instruments of the colonies, the following are well known historical facts: Lord Baltimore secured the charter for a Maryland colony in order that he and his associates might continue their Catholic worship free from Protestant persecution. Roger Williams, exiled from Massachusetts because of his religious views, established an independent colony in Rhode Island. The Huguenots, driven from France by the Edict of Nantes, sought in the more southern colonies a place where they could live in the enjoyment of their Huguenot faith.

It is not exaggeration to say that Christianity in some of its creeds was the principal cause of the settlement of many of the colonies, and cooperated with business hopes and purposes in the settlement of the others. Beginning in this way and under these influences it is not strange that the colonial life had an emphatic Christian tone.

The Constitution of Massachusetts of 1780 — which became the inspiration for the U.S. Constitution — included a provision for the public support for the "public worship of God."

From the very first efforts were made, largely it must be conceded by Catholics, to bring the Indians under the influence of Christianity. Who can read without emotion the story of Marquette, and others like him, enduring all perils and dangers and toiling through the forests of the west in their efforts to tell the story of Jesus to the savages of North America?

Within less than one hundred years from the landing at Jamestown three colleges were established in the colonies; Harvard in Massachusetts, William and Mary in Virginia and Yale in Connecticut. The first seal used by Harvard College had as a motto, *In Christi Gloriam*, and the charter granted by Massachusetts Bay contained this recital: "Whereas,

through the good hand of God many well devoted persons have been
and daily are moved and stirred up to give and bestow sundry gifts …
that may conduce to the education of the English and Indian youth of
this country, in knowledge and godliness."

The charter of William and Mary, reciting that the proposal was "to
the end that the Church of Virginia may be furnished with a seminary
of ministers of the gospel, and that the youth may be piously educated
in good letters and manners, and that the Christian faith may be propa-
gated amongst the western Indians, to the glory of Almighty God,"
made the grant "for propagating the pure gospel of Christ, our only Me-
diator, to the praise and honor of Almighty God." The charter of Yale
declared as its purpose to fit "young men for public employment both
in church and civil state," and it provided that the trustees should be
Congregational ministers living in the colony.

A Matter of Public Charge

In some of the colonies, particularly in New England, the support of
the church was a matter of public charge, even as the common schools
are today. Thus the Constitution of Massachusetts, of 1780, Part I, Article
3, provided that "the legislature shall, from time to time, authorize and
require the several towns, parishes, precincts, and other bodies politic or
religious societies to make suitable provision at their own expense for
the institution of the public worship of God and for the support and
maintenance of Protestant teachers of piety, religion and morality in all
cases where such provision shall not be made voluntarily."

Article 6 of the Bill of Rights of the Constitution of New Hampshire, of 1784, repeated in the Constitution of 1792, empowered "the legislature to authorize from time to time, the several towns, parishes,
bodies corporate, or religious societies within this State, to make ade-
quate provision at their own expense for the support and maintenance
of public Protestant teachers of piety, religion and morality."

In the fundamental Constitutions of 1769, prepared for the Carolinas by the celebrated John Locke, Article 96 reads: "As the country
comes to be sufficiently planted and distributed into fit divisions, it
shall belong to the parliament to take care for the building of churches,
and the public maintenance of divines to be employed in the exercise of
religion according to the Church of England, which being the only true
and orthodox and the national religion of all the king's dominions, is so

also of Carolina, and, therefore, it alone shall be allowed to receive public maintenance by grant of parliament."

In Maryland, by the Constitution of 1776, it was provided that "the legislature may, in their discretion, lay a general and equal tax, for "the support of the Christian religion."

In several colonies and states, a profession of the Christian faith was made an indispensable condition to holding office. In the frame of government for Pennsylvania, prepared by William Penn, in 1683, it was provided that "all treasurers, judges and other officers ... and all members elected to serve in provincial council and general assembly, and all that have right to elect such members, shall be such as profess faith in Jesus Christ."

And in the charter of privileges for that colony, given in 1701 by William Penn and approved by the colonial assembly, it was provided "that all persons who also profess to believe in Jesus Christ, the Savior of the World, shall be capable ... to serve this government in any capacity, both legislatively and executively."

In Delaware, by the Constitution of 1776, every officeholder was required to make and subscribe to the following declaration: "I, A. B., do profess faith in God the Father, and in Jesus Christ His Only Son, and in the Holy Ghost, one God, blessed forevermore; and I do acknowledge the Holy Scriptures of the Old and New Testament to be given by divine inspiration."

New Hampshire Provision

New Hampshire, in the Constitutions of 1784 and 1792, required that senators and representatives should be of the "Protestant religion," and this provision remained in force until 1877.

The fundamental Constitutions of the Carolinas declared: "No man shall be permitted to be a freeman of Carolina, or to have any estate or habitation within it that doth not acknowledge a God, and that God is publicly and solemnly to be worshiped."

The Constitution of North Carolina, of 1776, provided: "That no person who shall deny the being of God or the truth of the Protestant religion, or the divine authority either of the Old or New Testaments, or who shall hold religious principles incompatible with the freedom and safety of the State, shall be capable of holding any office or place of trust or profit in the civil department within this State." And this remained in force until 1835, when it was amended by changing the word "Protestant" to "Christian," and as so amended remained in force until the Constitution of 1868. And in that Constitution among the persons disqualified for office were "all persons who shall deny the being of Almighty God."

New Jersey, by the Constitution of 1776, declared "that no Protestant inhabitant of this colony shall be denied the enjoyment of any civil right merely on account of his religious principles, but that all persons professing a belief in the faith of any Protestant sect, who shall demean themselves peaceably under the government as hereby established, shall be capable of being elected into any office of profit or trust, or being a member of either branch of the legislature."

The Constitution of South Carolina, of 1776, provided that no person should be eligible to the House of Representatives "unless he be of the Protestant religion."

Massachusetts, in its Constitution of 1780, required from governor, lieutenant-governor, councilor, senator and representative before proceeding to execute the duties of his place or office a declaration that "I believe the Christian religion, and have a firm persuasion of its truth."

By the fundamental orders of Connecticut, the governor was directed to take an oath to "further the execution of justice according to the rule of God's word; so help me God, in the name of the Lord Jesus Christ."

The Vermont Constitution of 1777 required of every member of the House of Representatives that he take this oath: "I do believe in one God, the creator and governor of the universe, the rewarder of the good and punisher of the wicked, and I do acknowledge the scriptures of the Old and New Testaments to be given by divine inspiration, and own and profess the Protestant religion." A similar requirement was provided by the Constitution of 1786.

In Maryland, by the Constitution of 1776, every person appointed to any office of profit or trust was not only to take an official oath of allegiance to the State, but also to "subscribe a declaration of his belief in the Christian religion."

In the same State, in the Constitution of 1851, it was declared that no other test or qualification for admission to any office of trust or profit shall be required than the official oath "and a declaration of belief in the Christian religion; and if the party shall profess to be a Jew the declaration shall be of his belief in a future state of rewards and punishments."

As late as 1864 the same State in its Constitution had a similar provision, the change being one merely of phraseology, the provision reading, "a declaration of belief in the Christian religion, or of the existence of God, and in a future state of rewards and punishments."

Mississippi, by the Constitution of 1817, provided that "no person who denies the being of God or a future state of rewards and punishments shall hold any office in the civil department of the State."

CHAPTER 2:

Sundays Excepted

A nother significant matter is the recognition of Sunday. That day is the Christian Sabbath, a day peculiar to that faith, and known to no other. It would be impossible within limits of a lecture to point out all the ways in which that day is recognized. The following illustrations must suffice:

By the United States Constitution the President is required to approve all bills passed by Congress. If he disapproves he returns it with his veto. And then, specifically, it is provided that if not returned by him within ten days, "Sundays excepted," after it shall have been presented to him it becomes a law. Similar provisions are found in the Constitutions of most of the States, and in thirty-six out of forty-five is the same expression, "Sundays excepted."

Louisiana is one of the nine States in whose present Constitution the expression "Sundays excepted" is not found. Four earlier Constitutions of that State (those of 1812, 1845, 1852 and 1864) contained the phrase, while the three later ones, 1868, 1879 and 1881 omit those words.

If Sunday Intervenes

In *State ex rel. vs. Secretary of State*, a case arising under the last Constitution, decided by the Supreme Court of Louisiana (52 La. An. 936), the question was presented as to the effect of a governor's veto which was returned within time if a Sunday intervening between the day of presentation of the bill and the return of the veto was excluded. And too late if it was included; the burden of the contention on the one side being that the change in the phraseology of the later Constitutions in omitting the words "Sundays excepted" indicated a change in the meaning of the constitutional provision in respect to the time of a veto. The court unanimously held that the Sunday was to be excluded. In the course of its opinion it said (p. 944):

"In law Sundays are generally excluded as days upon which the performance of any act demanded by the law is not required. They are held to be *dies non juridici*.

"And in the Christian world Sunday is regarded as the 'Lord's Day,' and a holiday, a day of cessation from labor.

"By statute, enacted as far back as 1838, this day is made in Louisiana one of 'public rest.' Rev. Stat, Sec. 522; Code of Practice, 207, 763.

"This is the policy of the State of long standing, and the framers of the Constitution are to be considered as intending to conform to the same."

By express command of Congress, studies are not pursued at the military or naval academies, and distilleries are prohibited from operation on Sundays, while chaplains are required to hold religious services once at least on that day.

By the English statute of 29 Charles II no tradesman, artificer, workman, laborer, or other person was permitted to do or exercise any worldly labor, business or work of ordinary calling upon the Lord's Day, or any part thereof,

In some state constitutions during America's founding years, anyone denying the existence of God was disqualified from holding office.

works of necessity or charity only excepted. That statute, with some variations, has been adopted by most if not all the States of the Union.

In Massachusetts it was held that one injured while traveling in the cars on Sunday, except in case of necessity or charity, was guilty of contributory negligence and could recover nothing from the railroad company for the injury he sustained. And this decision was affirmed by the Supreme Court of the United States. A statute of the State of Georgia, making the running of freight trains on Sunday a misdemeanor, was also upheld by that court. By decisions in many States, a contract made

This painting depicts a Revolutionary War chaplain distributing Bibles to the soldiers. In September of 1777 Congress ordered 20,000 Bibles imported for use by the Army.

on Sunday is invalid and cannot be enforced. By the general course of decision no judicial proceedings can be held on Sunday.

All legislative bodies, whether municipal, state or national, abstain from work on that day. Indeed, the vast volume of official action, legislative and judicial, recognizes Sunday as a day separate and apart from the others, a day devoted not to the ordinary pursuits of life.

It is true in many of the decisions that this separation of the day is said to be authorized by the police power of the State and exercised for purposes of health. At the same time, through a large majority of them, there runs the thought of its being a religious day, consecrated by the Commandment, "Six days shalt thou labor, and do all thy work: but the seventh day is the Sabbath of the Lord thy God: in it thou shalt not do any work, thou, nor thy son, nor thy daughter, thy man servant, nor thy maid servant, nor thy cattle, nor the stranger that is within thy gates."

Grateful to Almighty God

While the word "God" is not infrequently used both in the singular and plural to denote any supreme being or beings, when used alone and in the singular number it generally refers to that Supreme Being spoken of in the Old and New Testaments and worshiped by Jew and Christian. In that sense the word is used in constitution, statute and instrument. In many State Constitutions we find in the preamble a declaration like this: "Grateful to Almighty God."

In some, he who denied the being of God was disqualified from holding office. It is again and again declared in constitution and statute that official oaths shall close with an appeal, "So help me, God." When, upon inauguration, the President-elect each four years consecrates himself to the great responsibilities of Chief Executive of the republic, his vow of consecration in the presence of the vast throng filling the Capitol grounds will end with the solemn words, "So help me, God." In all our courts witnesses in like manner vouch for the truthfulness of their testimony. The common commencement of wills is "In the name of God, Amen." Every foreigner attests his renunciation of allegiance to his former sovereign and his acceptance of citizenship in this republic by an appeal to God.

These various declarations in charters, constitutions and statutes indicate the general thought and purpose. If it be said that similar declarations are not found in all the charters or in all the constitutions, it will be borne in mind that the omission oftentimes was because they were deemed unnecessary, as shown by the quotation just made from the opinion of the Supreme Court of Louisiana, as well as those hereafter taken from the opinions of other courts. And further, it is of still more significance that there are no contrary declarations.

In no charter or constitution is there anything to even suggest that any other than the Christian is the religion of this country. In none of them is Mohammed or Confucius or Buddha in any manner noticed. In none of them is Judaism recognized other than by way of toleration of its special creed. While the separation of church and state is often affirmed, there is nowhere a repudiation of Christianity as one of the institutions as well as benedictions of society.

In short, there is no charter or constitution that is either infidel, ag nostic or anti-Christian. Wherever there is a declaration in favor of any religion it is of the Christian. In view of the multitude of expressions in its favor, the avowed separation between church and state is a most satisfactory testimonial that it is the religion of this country, for a peculiar thought of Christianity is of a personal relation between man and his Maker, uncontrolled by and independent of human government.

Why Chaplains?

Notice also the matter of chaplains. These are appointed for the army and navy, named as officials of legislative assemblies, and universally they belong to one or other of the Christian denominations. Their whole range of service, whether in prayer or preaching, is an official recognition of Christianity. If it be not so, why do we have chaplains?

If we consult the decisions of the courts, although the formal question has seldom been presented because of a general recognition of its truth, in *The People vs. Ruggles*, 8 John. 290, 294, 295, Chancellor Kent, the great commentator on American law, speaking as Chief Justice of the Supreme Court of New York, said: "The people of this State, in common with the people of this country, profess the general doctrines of Christianity, as the rule of their faith and practice." And in the famous case of Vidal vs. Girard's Executors, 2 How. 127, 198, the Supreme Court of the United States, while sustaining the will of Mr. Girard, with its provision for the creation of a college into which no minister should be permitted to enter, observed: "It is also said, and truly, that the Christian religion is a part of the common law of Pennsylvania."

The New York Supreme Court, in Lindenmuller vs. The People, 33 Barbour, 561, held that: "Christianity is not the legal religion of the State, as established by law. If it were, it would be a civil or political institution, which it is not; but this is not inconsistent with the idea that it is in fact, and ever has been, the religion of the people. This fact is everywhere prominent in all our civil and political history and has been, from the first, recognized and acted upon by the people, as well as by constitutional conventions, by legislatures and by courts of justice."

The South Carolina Supreme Court, in State vs. Chandler, 2 Harrington, 555, citing many cases, said:

Blasphemy Offenses

"It appears to have been long perfectly settled by the common law that blasphemy against the Deity in general, or a malicious and wanton attack against the Christian religion individually, for the purpose of exposing its doctrines to contempt and ridicule, is indictable and punishable as a temporal offense."

And again, in City Council vs. Benjamin, 2 Strobhart, 521:

"On that day we rest, and to us it is the Sabbath of the Lord; its decent observance in a Christian community is that which ought to be expected."

"It is not perhaps necessary for the purposes of this case to rule and hold that the Christian religion is part of the common law of South Carolina. Still it may be useful to show that it lies at the foundation of even the article of the Constitution under consideration, and that upon it rest many of the principles and usages, constantly acknowledged and enforced, in the courts of justice."

The Pennsylvania Supreme Court, in Updegraph vs. The Commonwealth, Sergeant and Rawle, 400, made this declaration:

"Christianity, general Christianity, is, and always has been, a part of the common law of Pennsylvania; Christianity, without the spiritual artillery of European countries; for this Christianity was one of the considerations of the royal charter, and the very basis of its great founder, William Penn; not Christianity founded on any particular religious tenets; not Christianity with an established church, and tithes, and spiritual courts; but Christianity with liberty of conscience to all men."

And subsequently, in *Johnson vs. The Commonwealth*, 10 Harris, III:

"It is not our business to discuss the obligations of Sunday any further than they enter into and are recognized by the law of the land. The common law adopted it, along with Christianity, of which it is one of the bulwarks."

In Arkansas, Shover vs. The State, 10 English, 263, the Supreme Court stated that:

"Sunday or the Sabbath is properly and emphatically called the Lord's Day, and is one amongst the first and most sacred institutions of the Christian religion. This system of religion is recognized as constituting a part and parcel of the common law, and as such all of the institutions growing out of it, or in any way, connected with it, in case they shall not be found to interfere with the rights of conscience, are entitled to the most profound respect, and can rightfully claim the protection of the law-making power of the State."

"While creeds and dogmas and denominations are in a certain sense losing their power, and certainly their antagonisms, yet as a vital force in the land, Christianity is still the mighty factor."

The Supreme Court of Maryland, in *Judefind vs. The State*, 78 Maryland, 514, declared:

"The Sabbath is emphatically the day of rest, and the day of rest here is the Lord's Day or Christian's Sunday. Ours is a Christian community, and a day set apart as the day of rest is the day consecrated by the resurrection of our Savior, and embraces the twenty-four hours next ensuing the midnight of Saturday. But it would scarcely be asked of a court, in what professes to be a Christian land, to declare a law unconstitutional because it requires rest from bodily labor on Sunday (except works of necessity and charity) and thereby promotes the cause of Christianity."

If now we pass from the domain of official action and recognition to that of individual acceptance, we enter a field of boundless extent, and I can only point out a few of the prominent facts:

Notice our educational institutions. I have already called your attention to the provisions of the charters of the first three colleges.

Think of the vast number of academies, colleges and universities scattered through the land. Some of them, it is true, are under secular control, but there is yet to be established in this country one of those institutions founded on the religions of Confucius, Buddha or Mohammed, while an overwhelming majority are under the special direction and control of Christian teachers.

Notice also the avowed and pronounced Christian forces of the country, and here I must refer to the census of 1890, for the statistics of the census of 1900 in these matters have not been compiled: The population was 62,622,000. There were 165,000 Christian church organizations, owning 142,000 buildings, in which were sittings for 40,625,000 people. The communicants in these churches numbered 20,476,000 and the value of the church property amounted to $669,876,000. In other words, about one third of the entire population were directly connected with Christian organizations.

Nearly two-thirds would find seats in our churches. If to the members we add the children and others in their families more or less connected with them, it is obvious that a large majority were attached to the various church organizations.

I am aware that the relationship between many members and their churches is formal, and that church relations do not constitute active and paramount forces in their lives, and yet it is clear that there is an identification of the great mass of American citizens with the Christian church. It is undoubtedly true that there is no little complaint of the falling off in church attendance, and of a luke-warmness on the part of many, and on the other hand there is a diversion of religious force along the lines of the Young Men's Christian Association, the Christian Endeavor Society and the Epworth League.

All these, of course, are matters to be noticed, but they do not avoid the fact of a formal adhesion of the great majority of our people to the Christian faith; and while creeds and dogmas and denominations are in a certain sense losing their power, and certainly their antagonisms, yet as a vital force in the land, Christianity is still the mighty factor. Connected with the denominations are large missionary bodies constantly busy in extending Christian faith through this nation and through the world. No other religious organization has anything of a foothold or is engaged in active work unless it be upon so small a scale

"On every hilltop towers the steeple of some Christian church, while from the marble witnesses in God's acre comes the universal but silent testimony to the common faith in the Christian doctrine of the resurrection and the life hereafter."

as scarcely to be noticed in the great volume of American life.

Again, the Bible is the Christian's book. No other book has so wide a circulation, or is so universally found in the households of the land. During their century of existence, the English and American Bible Societies have published and circulated two hundred and fifty million copies, and this represents but a fraction of its circulation. And then think of the multitude of volumes published in exposition, explanation and illustration of that book, or some portion of it.

You will have noticed that I have presented no doubtful facts. Nothing has been stated which is debatable. The quotations from charters are in the archives of the several States; the laws are on the statute books; judicial opinions are taken from the official reports; statistics from the census publications. In short, no evidence has been presented which is open to question.

I could easily enter upon another line of examination. I could point out the general trend of public opinion, the disclosures of purposes and beliefs to be found in letters, papers, books and unofficial declarations. I could show how largely our laws and customs are based upon the laws of Moses and the teachings of Christ; how constantly the Bible is appealed to as the guide of life and the authority in questions of morals;

how the Christian doctrines are accepted as the great comfort in times
of sorrow and affliction, and fill with the light of hope the services for
the dead. On every hilltop towers the steeple of some Christian church,
while from the marble witnesses in God's acre comes the universal but
silent testimony to the common faith in the Christian doctrine of the resurrection and the life hereafter.

But I must not weary you. I could go on indefinitely, pointing out
further illustrations both official and non-official, public and private;
such as the annual Thanksgiving proclamations, with their following
days of worship and feasting; announcements of days of fasting and
prayer; the universal celebration of Christmas; the gathering of millions
of our children in Sunday Schools, and the countless volumes of Christian literature, both prose and poetry.

But I have said enough to show that Christianity came to this country with the first colonists; has been powerfully identified with its rapid
development, colonial and national, and today exists as a mighty factor
in the life of the republic. This is a Christian nation, and we can all rejoice as truthfully we repeat the words of Leonard Bacon:

"O God, beneath thy guiding hand
Our exiled fathers crossed the sea,
And when they trod the wintry strand,
With prayer and psalm they worshiped Thee.

"Thou heardst, well pleased, the song, the prayer
Thy blessing came; and still its power
Shall onward through all ages bear
The memory of that holy hour.

"Laws. freedom, truth, and faith in God
Came with those exiles o'er the waves,
And where their pilgrim feet have trod,
The God they trusted guards their graves.

"And here Thy name, O God of love,

Their children's children shall adore,
Till these eternal hills remove,
And spring adorns the earth no more."

Part 2:
Our Duty As Citizens

CHAPTER 3:

Christianity and Patriotism

I considered last night the proposition that the United States of America is a Christian nation. I pointed out that Christianity was a primary cause of the first settlement on our shores; that the organic instruments, charters and constitutions of the colonies were filled with abundant recognitions of it as a controlling factor in the life of the people; that in one of them, at the least, it was in terms declared the established religion; while in several the furthering of Christianity was stated to be one of the purposes of the government.

In many, faith in it was a condition of holding office; in some, authority was given to the legislature to make its support a public charge; in nearly all the constitutions there have been express recognitions of the sanctity of the Christian Sunday; the God of the Bible is appealed to again and again. Sunday laws have been enacted and enforced in most of the colonies and States.

Our Christian Landscape

About one-third of the population are avowedly Christian and communicants in some Christian organization; there are sitting accommodations in the churches for nearly two-thirds; educational institutions are largely under the control of Christian denominations, and even in those which, in obedience to the rule of separation between church and state, are secular in their organization, the principles of Christianity are uniformly recognized.

By these and other evidences I claim to have shown that the calling of this republic a Christian nation is not a mere pretense, but a recognition of an historical, legal and social truth.

I come this evening to consider the consequences of this fact and the duties it imposes upon all our citizens.

And first, let it be noticed that there is no incompatibility between Christianity and patriotism. The declaration of the Master, "Render therefore unto Caesar, the things which are Caesar's; and unto God, the

This well-known brass engraving is on the side of the Federal Building in New York. It depicts General George Washington in prayer at Valley Forge during the harsh winter of 1778. One year later Washington ordered his troops to pray and to mention "our gracious redeemer," the "light of the gospel," "the church," "the light of Christian knowledge" and "the Holy Spirit." (Photo: Shutterstock)

things that are God's," is not a declaration of antagonism between the two, but an affirmation of duty to each. Indeed, devotion to one generally goes hand in hand with loyalty to the other. When Havelock, the hero of Luck-now, died, most appropriate were the words of the English poet:

"Strew not on the hero's hearse
Garlands of a herald's verse:
Let us hear no words of Fame
Sounding loud a deathless name:
Tell us of no vauntful Glory

Shouting forth her haughty story.
All lifelong his homage rose
To far other shrine than those.
'In hoc signo,' pale nor dim,
Lit the battlefield for him,
And the prize he sought and won,
Was the crown for duty done."

But we need not go elsewhere. In our own land, from the very first, Christianity and patriotism have worked together. When the Pilgrim Fathers touched New England's shores their first service was one of thanksgiving and praise to that Infinite One who had, as they believed, guided them to their new home.

In the long struggles of the early colonists with their Indian foes, the building on the hill was both church and fort. They fell on their knees and then on the aborigines, was the old satire, to which now is added, they fall on the Chinese.

In the convention that framed the Constitution, when doubt and uncertainty hovered over the result, at Franklin's insistance prayer was offered for the success of their efforts. In the dark days at Valley Forge the great leader sought strength and inspiration in prayer.

When the nation stood aghast at the assassination of Abraham Lincoln, the clarion voice of Garfield rang out above the darkness and the tumult, "God reigns; and the government at Washington still lives." And so I might go on with illustration after illustration showing how the faith of the Christian has stood in times of trial and trouble as the rock upon which the nation has rested.

Again, Christianity is entitled to the tribute of respect. I do not of course mean that all individuals, nominally Christian, deserve trust, confidence, or even respect, for the contrary is too often the case. Too often men hold religion as they do property, in their wives' names.

CHAPTER 4:

Give Honor Where Due

C hristianity is by no means beyond the reach of criticism and opposition. It is not lifted up as something too sacred to be spoken of save in terms and tones of reverence. This is an iconoclastic and scientific age. We are destroying many beliefs and traditions. William Tell is a myth. The long hairs of Pocahontas never dropped in protecting folds over the body of John Smith. The Arabs never destroyed the great library at Alexandria, though if some wandering Arabs would destroy all the law books in the land they would bless the courts and help the cause of justice.

We challenge the truthfulness of every assertion of fact, every de-

> *"Shall it be said that (Christianity) alone of all our benedictions has forfeited a claim to receive from every American citizen the tribute of respect?"*

mand upon our faith and confidence; and Christianity must stand like all other institutions, to be challenged, criticized, weighed and its merits and demerits determined. The time has passed in the history of the world when anything is too sacred to be touched, when anything is beyond the reach of the inquiring and scientific spear.

But while conceding all this, I insist that Christianity has been so wrought into the history of this republic, so identified with its growth and prosperity, has been and is so dear to the hearts of the great body of our citizens, that it ought not to be spoken of contemptuously or treated with ridicule.

Religion of any form is a sacred matter. It involves the relation of the individual to some Being believed to be infinitely supreme. It involves not merely character and life here, but destiny hereafter, and as such is not to be spoken of lightly or flippantly. And we who are citizens of this republic, recognizing the identification of Christianity with its life, the general belief that Christianity is the best of all religions, that it passed into the lives of our fathers and is taken into the lives of our brethren as something of sacred power, ought, even if not agreeing with all that is claimed for it, to at least accord to it respect.

I once listened to a conversation which illustrates my thought. It was between two young men returning after the close of a summer's vacation to the college at which both were students. The principal talker was, as I discovered in the course of the afternoon, an only son. On his upper lip was the first dark shadow of a coming mustache. He possessed that peculiar wisdom which belongs in this world to only the college sophomore. He was expressing to his companion his views on the Bible and religion, said he knew too much to believe in either; admitted that his mother believed in both and read her Bible every day; said that that might do for women and children, but not for any intelligent man in the light of present scientific knowledge.

You would have thought that Darwin and Huxley and Lord Kelvin had studied at his feet and that he was the Gamaliel of the present day. It is impossible to reproduce in language the self-sufficient sneering tone in which he spoke of the Bible, classing it with nursery rhymes, the story of Jack and the Beanstalk and the like, and the complacent pity with which he referred to those who were foolish enough to regard it as a sacred book. It is to be hoped that the budding sophomore lived long enough to learn that no gentleman speaks sneeringly of that which has been the lifelong faith and comfort of his mother.

Ode to the Flag

From the standpoint of citizenship, the treatment of Christianity may be regarded as in some respects similar to that which is accorded and is due to the national flag. Who looks upon that as a mere piece of cloth costing but a trifle, something to be derided or trampled upon at will? A particular banner may not have cost much. It may be cheap to him who sees only the material and work which have passed into it, but to every patriot it is the symbol of patriotism.

Its history is a record of glory. A century ago the Barbary pirates, who had defied the flags of Europe, saw it waving over Decatur's vessels and bowed in submission. Commodore Perry sailed beneath it into the unknown harbors of Japan, opened that nation to the nineteenth century, and today her civilization and power command universal respect and admiration. The oppressed Cuban appealed to it for deliverance, and in response thereto Manila and Santiago de Cuba introduced a new sister into the family of nations.

> "Wherever man has dared to go,
> 'Mid tropic heat or polar snow,
> On sandy plain or lofty crag,
> Has waved our country's starry flag.
> In that far North where ceaseless cold
> Has built its alabaster hold,
> And where the sun disdains to show
> His brightness on unbroken snow,
> Where icy pillars tower to heaven
> Pale sentinels to nature given,
> To watch the only spot she can
> Withhold from grasping hand of man,
> There Kane unfurled this banner bright,
> Resplendent with auroral light."

Today it waves at the masthead of American vessels in every water of the globe, and commands the world's respect. An insult to it every citizen feels is an insult to himself, and all insist that it shall be accorded due respect. We remember how, in the early days of our great civil struggle, the loyal heart was stirred with the thrilling words of Secretary Dix, "If any man attempts to haul down the American flag, shoot him on the spot." We honor Stonewall Jackson, who, seeing Barbara Frietchie waving this banner from the window of her home in Frederick, and the threatening guns of his soldiers, called out:

> " 'Who touches a hair of yon gray head
> Dies like a dog. March on,' he said."

We rejoice that now it floats in peace and triumph over all our fair land. We love to watch its fold swings out to the breeze on every patriotic day, to see it decorate the walls where gather our great conventions. We glory in every tribute that is paid to it in any part of the globe. It tells the story of conflicts, of defeats and victories. It has waved over many a field of battle, and the blood of our noblest and best has been shed in its defense. It is eloquent of all the sufferings and trials of days gone by, of all the great achievements of the American people, and as we swing it to the breeze we do so with undoubting faith that it will wave over grander things in the future of this republic.

Christianity has entered into and become part of the life of this republic; it came with its beginnings and prompted them; has been identified with its toils and trials, shared in its victories, cheered in the hour of darkness and gloom, and stands today prophetic of untold blessings in the future. And shall it be said that it alone of all our benedictions has forfeited a claim to receive from every American citizen the tribute of respect?

Respect for Christianity implies respectful treatment of its institutions and ordinances. This does not require that everyone must conform his life to those institutions and ordinances. That is something which each one has a right to settle for himself. Take, for instance, the matter of church services. No one is in duty bound as a citizen to attend a particular church service, or indeed any church service. The freedom of conscience, the liberty of the individual, gives to every individual the right to attend or stay away. At the same time there is an obligation not to unnecessarily interfere with or disturb those services. This is something more than the duty which rests upon one attending those services to avoid the ungentlemanly and unseemly act of disturbing the exercises. That is only a part of the common courtesy of all going into a gathering assembled for any lawful purpose.

They who call the meeting and who are engaged in service of any legitimate character have a right to be free from annoyance and interference. But beyond that the citizen who does not attend, does not even share in the belief of those who do, ought ever to bear in mind the noble part Christianity has taken in the history of the republic, the great share it has had in her wonderful development and its contribution to her present glory, and by reason thereof take pains to secure to those who do believe in it and do attend its services freedom from all disturbance of their peaceful gathering. The American Christian is entitled to his quiet hour.

Take another illustration, Sunday. Its separation from the other days as a day of rest is enforced by the legislation of nearly all if not all the States of the union.

Beyond that it is to the Christian a sacred day. It does not follow that it is the duty of every individual to observe the Sabbath as Christians do. Indeed, there is no unanimity of view among the latter as to the manner in which it should be observed. We have gone far away from the Puritan Sabbath and the austere, severe observance of it which prevailed in the early days of New England colonies, and which made the day a terror to children as well as burdensome to adults.

A Welcome Day

I believe it is conceded that notwithstanding the fabled blue laws of New England, a man may without impropriety kiss his wife on Sunday and possibly, if he have a chance, some other sweet-faced woman. That old time terror has been superseded by gentler and kindlier modes of observance, which tend to make the day welcome to all, both young and old, one in which is not merely rest from the ordinary toils of the week, but one in which the companionship of friends, the sweet influences of nature, and lessons from the higher forms of music and other arts are recognized as among its benedictions.

While the latter modes, though very likely more helpful, more really Christian, are a great departure from the former, it still remains true that it is a day consecrated of old, a day separated by law and religion as well as by the custom of the church for ages, and ought not to be turned into a day of public frivolity and gayety. While it may be true that all are not under obligations to conform to the higher and better uses of the day, yet at least they owe that respect to Christianity to pursue their frivolities and gaieties in such a way as not to offend those who believe in its sacredness.

I recognize the fact that it is not always easy to draw the line and that freedom implies not merely the freedom of those who would keep the day sacred, but also the freedom of those who do not so regard it.

Again, it deserves the attention and study of every citizen. You are all patriots, you love your country, are proud of its past and mean to so live and act that you can help it to the best possible future. Now, as I have pointed out, Christianity was a principal cause of the settlements on these western shores. It has been identified with the growth and development of those settlements into the United States of America, has so largely shaped and molded it that today of all the nations in the world it is the most justly called a Christian nation.

In order to determine what we ought to do for the future of the republic we must review its history, inquire into the causes which have made its growth and influenced its life, ascertained which have been the most controlling and which have helped on the better side of its development, and why they have been so influential.

CHAPTER 5:

A Positive Influence

I have shown that Christianity has been a great factor, and the student of our history will find that it has been a helpful and uplifting factor. Making full allowance for all the imperfections and mistakes which have attended it, as they attend all human institutions, I am sure that the student will be convinced that its general influence upon our national life has been for the better.

It has always stood for purity of the home, and who doubts that our homes have been the centers of the holiest living. It is Mormonism, Mohammedanism and heathenism and not Christianity which have proclaimed polygamy and debased woman from the sacred place of wife to the lower level of concubine. It is not Christianity which has sustained the social evil. All through our history, colonial and national, the hope and ambition of every young man and woman has been for a home of their own, into which one husband and one wife shall enter, "and they twain shall be one flesh."

One of the sad features of city life today is the crowding into apartments, where the janitor is master of the house and the independence of the home life is only partially secured. The barracks around our great manufacturing establishments are freighted with equally sad significance. While admitting this temporary departure, we rejoice that this has been pre-eminently a land of homes, whether in the city, or village, or country. And the power which has ever stood in the land for the purity of home life has been a crown of glory to the republic.

The Golden Rule

It has stood for business honesty and integrity. Its proclamation has been the golden rule. Do unto others as you would they should do unto you, is a summons to honesty and fair dealing in all business, as well as other relations in life. The Master never suggested that ability to keep outside the penitentiary was a sufficient test of honesty.

It has stood for liberty and the rights of man. In the great revolutionary struggle, the trusted counselors of the people were the preachers. While they may not be known in history as the leaders, were not the lawyers to draft the statutes and the constitution, nor the military heroes to command the armies, yet the local centers of influence were the Christian churches, and the Christian preachers were the men who kept the mass of the people loyal to the leadership of Washington and his associates.

And in the later struggle for human liberty, Christianity was always on the advance line. Those of us who remember the antebellum days recall the bitter flings that were made against preachers in politics. That was significant of the recognized truth that they were leading the great mass of the loyal people on in that most

Frances Willard, president of the Woman's Christian Temperance Union, exemplifies one of the attributes for which Christianity has always stood: temperance. It has been Christians who have been the foremost advocates for a "sober and pure world by abstinence, purity and evangelical Christianity," according to the group's mission statement.

wonderful civil war of all the ages. That struggle, as everyone knows, commenced on the plains of Kansas, and the New England emigrant crossed those plains, singing the song of Whittier:

"We go to plant our common schools
On distant prairie swells,
And give the Sabbaths of the wild
The music of her bells.

"Up bearing like the ark of old,
The Bible in our van,
We go to test the truth of God
Against the fraud of man."

And all during the terrible days of the great war, from every Union camp and company rolled up the majestic music of the battle hymn of the republic:

"In the beauty of the lilies Christ was born across the sea, with a glory in his bosom that transfigures you and me: As he died to make men holy, let us die to make men free, While God is marching on."

It has stood for education. I have already called your attention to this matter in proof of the Christian character of the nation. It may be added that outside of the institutions with direct State support, nearly every academy, college and university was founded by and is under the control of some one of the several Christian denominations. Indeed, a frequent criticism of many is that they are too much under such control. Certain is it that they would never have come into being but for the denominations back of them.

Up to a recent date the rule was that the presidents and an exceedingly large majority of the faculty of all these institutions be ministers. It was a national surprise when first a layman was elected a college president. In the common schools the Bible has been as much a textbook as the New England primer. It is only within very late years that any objection has been raised to its daily use, and that objection has sprung as

"It is Mormonism, Mohammedanism and heathenism, and not Christianity, which have proclaimed polygamy and debased women from the sacred place of wife to the lower level of concubine."

much from differences between the Catholic and Protestant denominations concerning the version to be used as from opposition to the book itself.

It has stood for the great charities and benevolences of the land. What single organization has done more for the orphan than the Catholic Church? What one, through hospital and asylum, more for the sick and afflicted? If you were to select a single face and form as the typical expression of the great thought of charity and kindness, whose would you select other than the face and form of a Sister of Charity?

"The Little Sister of the Poor"

"Amid the city's dust and din
Your patient feet have trod;
Wherever sorrow is or sin
You do the work of God.

"You seem in many a shadowed place
A glory from above,
The peace of heaven is in your face,
And in your heart is love.

"Your brow is lined with others' cares,
And aches for others' needs;
You bless the dying with your prayers,
The living with your deeds.

"You sow the wayside hope that lives
Where else were only death;
Your love is like the rain that gives
Heaven's secret to the earth.

"The pitying thoughts that fill your eyes,
And rob your years of rest,
That lead you still where misery sighs
And life is all un-blest,

"Are as the tears that angels shed
O'er darkened lives forlorn
Stars in the gloom till night has fled,
And dew on earth at morn."

In times when epidemics rage, when death seems to haunt every city home, who are the devoted ones to risk their lives in caring for the sick and paying the last offices to the dead? Surely, as the vision of this rises in your mind, you see the presence and form of those whose faith is in the Man of Galilee.

It has stood for peace. I need not content myself by referring to that Christian denomination, one of whose distinguishing tenets is unqualified opposition to all wars. I can with safety point to the great body of those who in days gone by have been the champions of the cause of peace; to the memorials which have been presented to the two Houses of Congress in favor of arbitration; to those who are at the head of the various peace societies, and who are always found upon the platforms at their gatherings, and whose voices are most constant and potent in its behalf. Indeed, strike from the history of this country all that the Christian Church has done in the interest and to further the cause of peace and there is not as much life left as was found in the barren fig tree.

It has stood for temperance. Not that it has stood alone, but it has been a leader. The foremost advocates of the cause have been pronounced Christians. Frances Willard was president of the Woman's Christian Temperance Union, not of the Woman's Mohammedan Temperance Union, and the White Ribboners are not disciples of Confucius

"It has been often said that Christian nations are the civilized nations, and as often that the most thoroughly Christian are the most highly civilized. Is this a mere coincidence?"

or Buddha. The churches have been the places of the great gatherings of the friends of temperance. Indeed, when you survey the efforts made to further that cause you will find that, running through them all, Christianity has been distinctively present.

In short, it has sought to write into the history of this nation the glowing words of the apostle:

"Love, joy, peace, long-suffering, gentleness, goodness, faith, meekness, temperance; against such there is no law."

It has stood for all these things because they represent its thought and purpose. So, he who studies the history of the country, finding this to be the lesson of its influence upon our history, can but be led to the conclusion not merely that it has been a potent factor in the life of the nation, but also that it has been a healthful and helpful factor. When one who loves his country realizes this fact, does there not open before him a clear vision of his duty to further its influence? If in the past it has done so much and so well for the country, is there any reason to doubt that strengthened and extended it will continue the same healthful and helpful influence?

It has been often said that Christian nations are the civilized nations, and as often that the most thoroughly Christian are the most highly civilized. Is this a mere coincidence?

Cause and Effect

Study well the history of Christianity in its relation to the nation and it will be found that it is something more than a mere coincidence, that there is between the two the relation of cause and effect, and that the more thoroughly the principles of Christianity reach into and influence the life of the nation, the more certainly will that nation advance in civilization. At least it is the duty of every patriot, finding that it has been such a factor in our life, to inquire whether it does stand to its civilization in the relation of cause and effect, and it would be in the highest degree unphilosophical to assume that there has been only a coincidence, and therefore that its presence in the nation is a matter of indifference.

If found that it has been both a potent and helpful factor in the development of our civilization, then it is a patriot's duty to uphold it and extend its influence. This is in line with the general obligation which rests upon all to help everything which tends to the bettering of the life of the republic. Who does not recognize that obligation in other directions?

Today, prevalent belief is that in order to maintain our position in the world, a position which has rapidly changed from one of isolation to that of intimate relation with all nations, we ought to pay larger attention to our navy. If that belief is well founded, if it be true that a larger and more efficient navy is essential to the maintenance of our position in the world, then who will question the duty of every citizen?

May we antagonize that which the nation's interests demand? Shall we through selfishness or indifference permit that which means the wellbeing and glory of the nation to become weak or to fail altogether? Who hesitates about the answer to such a question? So with our commerce. Is it not a praiseworthy effort on the part of each and all to enlarge that commerce and thus to add to the prosperity which attends a successful world commerce?

Or to come closer to those things which touch the social and moral well-being of the nation, who doubts a patriot's duty to further the cause of education? Who questions that the best interests of the republic are prompted by extending education to all? And can anyone, doing justice to himself, and without violating his duty to the republic, plead that he is wholly indifferent to the matter?

Take another illustration: civil service reform. I shall not enter into any argument in its favor. I assume that the principle of it commends itself to the thoughtful as something which, wisely administered, will eliminate much of the pitiful scramble for office and secure a better administration of public affairs. Upon that assumption who does not feel that he has a duty in so far as in him lies to further the movement in its favor? It may be that it has not yet accomplished that which its friends believe it possible of accomplishing; that much is to be done before it is placed upon a permanent and efficient basis. And yet, if it be something which in its development will redound to the national wellbeing, is there not a duty resting upon all to strengthen and perfect it?

Now, these are mere illustrations of the duty which, as patriotic citizens, we all feel. Upon what grounds may we recognize our obligations in these directions and decline to do anything to extend and make more efficient the principles of Christianity?

A Citizen's Duty

I am not now presenting this as a question affecting the life hereafter. I am putting it before you simply as a citizen's duty; as a matter affecting only the wellbeing and glory of the republic. You may concede that, as illustrated by the lives of its professed followers, Christianity comes far short of what you think it ought to be, and yet if you believe that its spirit and principles are freighted with blessing to the individual, as well as to the nation, is it not an obvious duty to seek to purify it in the individual and strengthen it in the nation?

The selfish spirit is not a commendable element in the life of a true citizen. It is as old as scripture that no man liveth unto himself alone. In the marvelously and increasingly intimate relations of individuals one to the other and the growing power of the citizen over the life of the nation, the unselfish patriot must always consider not simply his own interests, his own comfort and convenience, but those things which make for the wellbeing of all.

The significance of this duty has another aspect. "No man liveth unto himself alone" may be broadened into "No nation liveth unto itself alone." Neighbor is no longer confined to the vocabulary of the individual. It is a national word. Modern inventions have annihilated distance. Commercial relations have broken down barriers of race and religion, and the family of nations is a recognized fact. This republic has joined in the movement of the age. She no longer lives an isolated life separated by the oceans from the great powers of the world. She sits in the councils of the nations and we rejoice to speak of her and hear her spoken of as a world power.

Indeed, some begin to think ambitiously of this republic as a sort of international policeman, with the right to exercise all the functions of a policeman in preserving order and keeping peace. The Monroe Doctrine is to be extended. No longer simply a prohibition upon further European colonies, but a declaration that if any European power claims anything from any nation on this hemisphere it must appeal to the United States and not attempt to assert by force its claims. We propose to administer the estate of San Domingo, even before its death. We intend to preserve the integrity of China. We intimated to Russia that the Jews must no longer be persecuted. We are disposed to say to Turkey that Armenian life and property must be safe, and we hear, as the Apostle of old, the cry, "Come over into Macedonia and help us."

I do not stop to discuss whether we are not overdoing in this direction, whether it is wise wholly to forget Washington's farewell advice to avoid entangling alliances with other nations. Neither shall I attempt to criticize the recently announced maxim of national duty, "speak softly, but carry a big stick."

But of one thing I am sure. In no other way can this republic become a world power in the noblest sense of the word than by putting into her life and the lives of her citizens the spirit and principles of the great founder of Christianity. We have faith in the future of the United States. We believe she will advance in many directions. She may increase her territory, add to her population, her commerce may grow larger, her accumulations in wealth surpass the wildest dreams of the Pilgrim Fathers, her inventive skill subject all the forces of nature to do her bidding and surround every home with comforts and luxuries unknown even to the present day.

Besides her statues and paintings the chiseled beauties of Phidias and the pictured splendors of Raphael may seem the works of tyros [novices], her literature may dwarf all the achievements of the writers and thinkers of ages past and thus she may tower in greatness in the sight of the world. But grander far, and far more potential over the nations will she be when the beatitudes become the Magna Carta of her life and her citizens live in full obedience to the Golden Rule. Then, and not until then, will all nations and their peoples join rejoicing with our citizens in this triumphal song to the great republic:

"Thou, too, sail on, oh Ship of State!
Sail on, oh, Union, strong and great!
Humanity with all its fears,
With all the hopes of future years,
Is hanging breathless on thy fate!
We know what Master laid thy keel,
What workmen wrought thy ribs of steel,
Who made each mast, and sail, and rope,
What anvils rang, what hammers beat,
In what a forge and what a heat
Were shaped the anchors of thy hope!
Fear not each sudden sound and shock,
'Tis of the wave and not the rock;
'Tis but the flapping of the sail.
And not a rent made by the gale!
In spite of rock and tempests roar,
In spite of false lights on the shore,
Sail on, nor fear to breast the sea!
Our hearts, our hopes, are all with thee,
Our hearts, our hopes, our prayers, our tears,
Our faith triumphant o'er our fears,
Are all with thee, are all with thee!"

Part 3:

The Promise and Possibilities of the Future

CHAPTER 6:

The Great Melting Pot

And now, what of the future? If Christianity has been so largely identified with the life of this nation and identified in a helpful and blessing way, what promise and possibilities does it bring of the future? Of course, whatever tends to the better life of the individual, helps to promote the welfare of the nation. Anything that conduces to personal purity, morality and integrity increases the same characteristics in the community.

It needs no declaration of scripture to convince that "righteousness exalteth a nation; but sin is a reproach to any people." Insofar, therefore, as the principles and precepts of Christianity develop righteousness in the individual, to the same extent will a similar result be found in the life of the nation. This subject in its general features opens the door to extended discussion and is susceptible of many illustrations. The contrast between the standard of life in a heathen and that in a Christian nation shows the range of examination into which we may enter.

Out of the wide field of illustration, let me call your attention to one or two matters in which the Christian character of this republic shines out with richest promise. One arises from the fact that this nation is composed of people of various races and not wholly or even substantially of one.

We all have read the story of the dispersion at Babel. That story may not be the narration of an actual experience, yet it is a correct foreshadowing of the world's history. In whatsoever way it commenced, through all the ages the inhabitants of the globe have been gathered in separate localities, each race or tribe occupying its own locality.

The history of the world is one long story of strife between nation and nation, tribe and tribe, race and race. And everywhere today, except here, we find within the territory of a nation one race alone, or so nearly alone, that it is supremely dominant. You go to Germany and the Germans are there, forming the substantial controlling part of the population. There may be a few foreigners engaged in business or travel, some may even make it their home, but it is a German nation pure and simple, and the other races have no place in its life. In France, Russia, Turkey, it is the same. But in this republic it is different, and no race monopolizes American life. The dispersion at Babel has ended on the banks of the Mississippi. And the races that once separated and have continued separate and

Newly arrived immigrants wait at Ellis Island. The "mingling of the races" in America is not by accident, asserts the author. (Photo: The Statue of Liberty-Ellis Island Foundation, Inc./National Park Service/Shutterstock)

antagonistic for untold centuries are mingling here in a common life.

While all doubtless have in a general way some notion of the many foreigners in our midst, few realize the extent to which this nation is made up of different races. Let me give a few figures taken from the census of 1900. The total population was 76,000,000 of which 67,000,000 were white, and 9,000,000 colored. That is one race, 9,000,000, out of the 76,000,000. Of the white population there were of native parentage 41,000,000, of foreign, 26,000,000. Of the latter, 10,000,000 were also of foreign birth; and when you speak of foreign parentage, you must remember that almost all of us, going back two or three generations, will find foreign ancestors. Of the 26,000,000 of foreign parentage there were (counting by hundreds of thousands) from Austria, 400,000; Bohemia, 400,000; Canada, 2,100,000; France, 300,000; Italy 700,000; Germany, 7,800,000; Hungary, 200,000; Ireland, 5,000,000; Norway, 800,000;

Poland, 700,000; Russia, 700,000; Scotland, 600,000; Sweden, 1,100,000; Switzerland, 300,000; Wales, 200,000; other nations, 1,100,000, and of mixed parentage, 1,300,000.

This multitude is here, not as travelers with a view of temporary sojourn, but to make this their home. They are invited under our law to become, and they do become, citizens, sharing with us the duties and responsibilities of citizenship so that we have gathered as members of our nation hundreds of thousands from almost every race on the face of the globe. They come, bringing with them that antagonism of race which has continued for centuries. The old quarrels are not forgotten. They bring with them differences in habits and thoughts, in political hopes and convictions, differences of religious faith, and in many instances a lack of any faith. They come and are merged into the life of this nation, and are, as you and I, to make its destiny. They form part of the forces which are to shape the future of this country.

Some think, or say they think, that there is no such thing as an overruling Providence, that we are mere atoms of matter tossed to and fro on the face of the earth, and that here is the beginning and the end. They do not take into thought the great life of the ages, or measure its movements from its first feeble steps; and yet they sometimes feel compelled to admit that it seems as though there were something more than mere blind chance.

I remember that Speaker Reed once said in a public address (I am not quoting his exact words) that while he himself was not much of a believer in special providences, it did seem as though

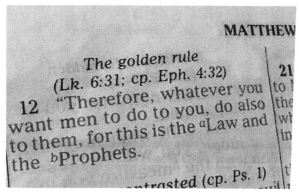

MATTHEW

The golden rule
(Lk. 6:31; cp. Eph. 4:32)

21

12 "Therefore, whatever you to want men to do to you, do also the to them, for this is the ⁿLaw and wh the ᵇProphets.

...trusted (cp. Ps. 1)

The Golden Rule is embodied in Christianity; it is an illustration of the "better life" offered through Christ.

these things referring to some of the great events of history were brought about by an intelligent and infinite Being. You may fancy that the mingling of all these races in this country is a mere accident; that it simply happened so. And yet if you will reflect a little you will be led to the conclusion that, as Tennyson writes:

"Through the ages one increasing purpose runs."

Four centuries ago the nations in the then-known world were living their isolated and separate lives. Racial antagonism was persistent. There was little intercourse between them. Education was practically unknown. There were a few learned men here and there. The common people were crushed to earth.

Dreaming of Liberty

Religion, the religion of Christ, was largely buried beneath a mass of superstitions. The Bible was a chained book. The world was creeping on through the darkness of the Middle Ages, and the morning seemed away off in the distance. Then Gutenberg invented printing. Luther said the Bible must be an open book. The masses began to read and dream of liberty. Columbus declared that there was a land away to the west; he journeyed in little caravels across the ocean, and America was discovered.

To the temperate part of this western continent came the Huguenot from France, the Pilgrim from England, the persecuted from different lands, and settled along the Atlantic shore. Religion was a potent factor in the settlement of these colonies. Now, is it not strange that by mere chance, printing, a free Bible, an unoccupied country, and an absorbing desire for greater liberty should come about the same time, and that as the outcome of this coincidence there should settle upon the virgin soil of this new continent colonies escaping from persecution and bringing here education, liberty and religion?

And then, is it not singular that to this new continent there should come through the years that followed, from every race on the face of the globe, a multitude seeking a new home, settling beneath the Stars and Stripes, feeling that in some way or other this was the place where the great destinies of the future were to be wrought out?

Is this all accidental? Does it not suggest that in the councils of eternity, long before man began to be, it was planned that here in this republic should be worked out the unity of the race, a unity made possible by the influences of education and the power of Christianity? Certainly, to me it is a supreme conviction, growing stronger and stronger as the years go by, that this is one purpose of Providence in the life of this republic, and that to this end we are to take from every race its strongest and best elements and characteristics, and mold and fuse them into one homogeneous American life.

Some of you know something about composite photography, and how face after face is thrown upon the same plate until a picture is produced which is a representation of thirty or forty faces, one upon another. As you look at this composite picture, you see that the marked and strong characteristics of each face are visible, while the weak ones are lost. America is the great national photographer. She takes from every race its best elements and is to mold them into one American character.

What does all this mean? If there be a purpose running through the life of the world, is it not plain that one thought in the divine plan was that in this republic should be unfolded and developed in the presence

> *"If there be a purpose running through the life of the world, is it not plain that one thought in the divine plan was that in this republic should be unfolded and developed in the presence of the world the Christian doctrine of the fatherhood of God and the brotherhood of man?"*

of the world the Christian doctrine of the fatherhood of God and the brotherhood of man?

To the full realization of this, something more is necessary than a mere uniting in the active duties of our daily life; something more than interracial marriages bringing the races into one common stock; something more than a mingling in toil, whether on the farm, in the shop, the factory or the office, the working together in the same political parties, or the prosecution of the same lines of study and identification in all material interests.

Beyond all this must be developed the essentials of a pure family life, a community of thought and purpose in those higher things which make for the betterment of all. It is not that here one race shall be enabled to rise to the fullest development of its capacity, while all other races are ministering to that uplifting, but rather that each and every one of every race should be given the amplest opportunity for his own elevation.

Open Door for Everyone

No perfect family exists where one is bound down with the lower duties in order that another shall rise. It exists only when each is given the fullest possible scope for his own uprising. There will always be diversity of work, but the open door must be before everyone.

For the realization of this can anything be more potent than the golden rule, the presence of the spirit of Christianity? Under its power each will be faithful in the work he does, while evermore to him is outstretched the helping hand of all.

And so it will be that all races mingling in the common American life will give to it of their best, and here, first of all, will be realized the fulfillment of the final prayer of the Master in the Upper Chamber:

"That they all may be one; as Thou, Father, art in me, and I in Thee."

Surely this republic may glory in the opportunity through its Christian life and power of winning for herself the great glory of such achievement.

CHAPTER 7:

Building a Better Mankind

A nother door of promise is open in the opportunity before
America of realizing within her borders the highest standard
of life. One of the pressing dangers facing all civilized nations
is the enervating influence of wealth and great material development.

That was the one thing which sapped the life of the great nations of
antiquity and buried them in the tombs of their own vices. In each there
was a wonderful accumulation of wealth, marvelous manifestations of
material splendor, but the moral character of their citizens was under-
mined thereby and they declined and fell.

The hanging gardens of Babylon, the pyramids of Egypt, the sculp-
tured beauty which lined the streets of Athens, and all that luxurious
display which attended the centering in Rome of the products of the
civilizations of the earth in their day provoked the admiration and were
the boast of their citizens. They passed through the same round of experience. Wealth brought luxury, luxury brought vice and vice was followed by ruin and decay. And now we dig through the accumulating
dust of centuries to find even the ruins of their vanished splendor.

'Marvelous Material Development'

Today we are in the presence of a like marvelous material development. It is one of the phenomena which attracts everybody's attention.
You hear on all sides descriptions of the wonderful things which the scientific mind and the ingenious skill of the country is accomplishing. The
skyscrapers, the tunnels, the railroads, the mighty steamships, the tele-
graph, the cable, the telephone, all these things, with their accompany-
ing conveniences and luxuries, are before us.

I am not here to say aught against the magnificence of this material
development, but, remember it is only a means to an end. We do not
live to make bricks and mortar, nor to build skyscrapers. You go on the
banks of the Nile and there, rivaling all that we have built, stand those
gloomy, lofty pyramids, as they have stood for century after century,
looking out over the silent sands, speaking no word to humanity of

cheer and encouragement, telling no tale of something done for the betterment of the race, and in their cold, sad solitude, witnesses only to unrequited toil in behalf of men whose names have almost vanished from history.

Macauley, in one of his beautiful essays, suggests that possibly the time may come when some South Sea Islander will stand on the broken arches of London Bridge, looking upon the deserted ruins of that city and wondering at the civilization that in it once prevailed.

"The better life rests less on the prohibitions of the Ten Commandments and more on the parable of the Good Samaritan and the Golden Rule." (Photo: Shutterstock)

The one thing that will save this country from the destiny which has attended those nations which have vanished into oblivion, which will make our marvelous material development something for the glory of humanity and the up building and permanence of this republic, is the putting into the life of the nation the conviction that the purpose and end of all is the building up of a better manhood and womanhood.

How is this to be accomplished? Not certainly by giving up all our thought to material development. "As a man thinketh, so is he." And if the nation puts all its energies and thought into simply the work of extending its commerce, improving its highways, building up great cities and adding to its manufactures, it may expect the fate which attended those departed nations.

Neither is it accomplished by any inculcation of the merely utilitarian philosophy of a selfish morality. Honesty undoubtedly is the best policy. It is a maxim, good in itself, but if the only thought is of the pecuniary results of such a policy it will fail. He who is honest in his dealings simply because of the social prestige and position it secures will never develop his higher nature, but will always live along the lower lines.

You must fill the soul with the impulses of the higher spirit of righteousness, the spirit that makes justice and uprightness things to be sought after because of their own blessed influences upon the individual. That is the spirit which is measured not by its capacity for coinage into dollars, but by its power upon the life.

The better life rests less on the prohibitions of the Ten Commandments and more on the parable of the Good Samaritan and the Golden Rule. The rich man who came to the Master declared in reference to the Commandments, "All these have I kept from my youth up," but his weakness was pierced by the searching reply, "One thing thou yet lackest; go sell whatsoever thou hast and follow me." In other words, Christianity, entering into the life of the individual, and thus into the life of the nation, is the only sure antidote for the poisonous touch of mere material prosperity.

Do you ever doubt the outcome, or dread to think of the possible future of the republic? Remember that "Behind the dim unknown, Standeth God within the shadow, keeping watch above His own."

The Gospel of Peace

Another illustration is in its influence for peace in the world. Christianity is called the gospel of peace. Among the names which in prophecy were ascribed to its founder is that of "Prince of Peace." At the time of his birth it is said that the doors of the Temple of Janus in Rome were closed by reason of the fact that peace, for the time being, prevailed in all the nations. Among the last words to his disciples in the upper chamber were, "Peace I leave with you." The dream of the warring world has ever been of the coming of a time when peace should prevail.

War, however just, however righteous, is attended with unspeakable horrors. All accept General Sherman's characterization that "war is hell." It is to the glory of this nation that it has already done so much in the interests of peace and to minimize the horrors of war.

In Jay's Treaty with Great Britain in 1794, there were stipulations against the confiscation of debts due from the individuals of the one nation to individuals of the other, and for the peaceful residence of citizens of either nation in the territory of the other during the continuance of the war.

At the time of the French Revolution, our government issued stringent orders in respect to the preservation of neutrality, so stringent as to call from Mr. Hall, the recent leading English writer on international law, the declaration that "the policy of the United States in 1793 constitutes an epoch in the development of the usages of neutrality."

During the administration of Mr. Monroe, our government proposed to France, England and Russia that, in times of war, merchant vessels and their cargoes belonging to subjects of belligerent powers should be exempt from capture. While we did not assent in 1856 to the Declaration of Paris, by which privateering was abolished, we offered to agree to it if the nations would consent that private property on the seas should be free from capture. Since then we have agreed to the abolition of privateering. The proclamations of our presidents at the commencements of recent wars and the decisions of our Supreme Court have been along the line of ameliorating the hardships of war.

We stood with Great Britain at The Hague Conference as the most earnest advocates of the establishment of an international arbitration tribunal. In the Orient, China and Japan each recognize this government as of all, the most free from selfish motives in its treatment of them and action for them. The integrity of China depends on this republic, and the territorial limits of the present war have been narrowed at our insistence.

Our international relations have been lifted from the lower to a higher plane. Diplomatic language is no longer a means of concealing, but of expressing thought and purpose. Neither Machiavelli nor Talleyrand is the type of American diplomacy.

Right Over Might

Does the day of peace seem a long way off? Think of the ages upon ages during which, even within the limits of a nation, with its compact and unifying forces, has been evolving the supremacy of right over might and the settlement of disputes by judicial action rather than physical force. We have no reason to expect a speedy coming of the day when the judicial function will settle all disputes between nations. A nation may be born in a day, but the great truths which make for the glory and uplift of the race only through long ages permeate and control humanity.

We must have the divine patience and understand the divine mathematics of a thousand years as one day. There will yet be wars and rumors of wars. Our own loved land will not be exempt. The cry for a larger navy will long be a party slogan. The air will be resonant with the blare of bugles. The tramp, tramp of armed battalions will be along our streets. Statues of our great commanders will be seen in all our parks and buildings, and present history will be filled with the story of military and naval achievements.

But the leaven of the immortal truth that right rather that might attests the ideal life is already working in the mass of humanity, and slowly it will leaven the whole lump.

I am not here to make light of the patriotic devotion of our mili-

> *"By common consent (Jesus) stands as the most potent individual force for the highest things of life."*

tary and naval heroes. I would not take one jot or tittle from all the glory which attends our army and navy and crowns with laurel its heroes. But at the same time I want to affirm my faith that the laurels of peace are more enduring than those of war. Time, which is the Almighty's great right hand of recompense, will brighten the one while it dims the other. John Marshall will be remembered when Winfield Scott is forgotten.

In the far off future the names of our greatest commanders will fill a lessening space in the horizon of history, while with ever brightening splendor will shine the name of America's peace-loving and golden-rule diplomat, Secretary John Hay.

The measure of fame will be meted out by Him who has declared that He will lay judgment to the line and righteousness to the plummet. Is not it a great thing to be a leader among the nations in the effort to bring on that day when the sword shall be beaten into the ploughshare and the spear into the pruning hook, and when war shall cease? And the more thoroughly this republic is filled with the spirit of the gospel, the more universal the rule of Christianity in the hearts of our people, the more certainly will she ever be the welcome leader in movements for peace among the nations.

Nineteen centuries ago there broke upon the startled ears of Judea's shepherds watching their flocks beside the village of Bethlehem, the only angel's song ever heard by the children of earth:

"It came upon the midnight clear,
That glorious song of old,
From angels bending near the earth
To touch their harps of gold:
'Peace on the earth. Good-will to men
From Heaven's all gracious king.' "

The air above Judea's plains no longer pulsates with the waves of this celestial song. For sad and weary centuries the march of humanity upwards has been through strife and blood. But a growing echo of the heavenly music is filling the hearts of men, and the time will come, the blessed time will come ...

"When the whole world gives back the song
Which now the angels sing."

One thing more. Whatever difference of opinion there may be as to the divinity of the Man of Galilee, His position as a man is confessedly supreme. Renan, the brilliant French writer, closed his life of Christ with these words:

"Whatever the unexpected phenomena of the future, Jesus will never be surpassed. His worship will constantly renew its youth, the legend of His life will bring ceaseless tears, his sufferings will soften the best hearts; all the ages will proclaim that, amongst the sons of men, none has been born who is greater than Jesus."

By common consent He stands as the most potent individual force for the highest things of life. Jesus was a Galilean youth, away from the centers of civilization, untaught in the schools, living a humble life among country people, familiar with poverty and having no place whereon to lay His head, dying at the age of thirty-three, after only three years of public presentation of Himself.

How strange that He made so little impression on the life of the world that only a single word or two respecting Him is found in the records of Rome, the great center of civilization. Now, after the lapse of nineteen centuries, He is revered as divine by millions upon millions, and is universally acknowledged as the most uplifting power known to humanity, whose power is ever widening until it touches all quarters of the globe.

The Highest Civilization

Faith in Him goes hand in hand with the highest civilization, and all realize that the more His spirit enters into one's life, the better that life becomes. In the light of this admitted fact, can anyone look thoughtfully upon the future of this nation without believing that if His spirit shall become more and more potent, not merely the individual citizens, but the nation as a whole, will rise in all the elements of moral grandeur and power?

With patriotic and prophetic vision we see our beloved country advancing, not alone along the lines of material prosperity and accumulating wealth, but also along the better lines of increasing intelligence and a loftier sense of duty. We see her quickened by the ennobling power of the golden rule, and the spirit of the Good Samaritan, bidding all her citizens to seek first the kingdom of God and its righteousness.

America has introduced into the vocabulary of international law the blessed word "neighbor," leading humanity along the kindly ways of peace and mutual helpfulness until "out of every kindred, and tongue, and people, and nation" shall rise a glad psalm of thanksgiving and joy that in the good providence of the Almighty there has been planted upon these western shores the living and growing tree of liberty, education and Christian principles.

Young gentlemen, to you, as to comparatively few in the long lapse of centuries, comes a magnificent opportunity. Before you is the open door to great achievement and great usefulness. With rich endowment of youth, health, friends and education you stand in the morning hours of that which is to be a century of unsurpassed significance.

We look back on the last fifty years as years of wonderful scientific development and marvelous inventions, yet Lord Kelvin, perhaps the greatest scientist of today, said in substance, not long since, that, wonderful as have been the accomplishments in these respects during those years, we are trembling on the verge of inventions and discoveries as far surpassing them as they do any that have gone before. That declaration coming from such a mind was, and is, prophetic. Since then wireless telegraphy has come, and who shall guess the next marvel?

The Spirit of Liberty

The spirit of liberty is shaking thrones and dynasties the world over, and making government of the people, by the people, and for the people a nearer fact. Even that great embodiment of despotism among civilized nations, Russia, is now rocking from one end to the other through its dynamic explosions.

Education is sweeping through the world and the common school is lifting the masses up to a higher level and a stronger citizenship. Engineering skill seems to know no limits. Time and space are abolished. Steam is slow and giving place to electricity. Gigantic combinations of capital grapple without hesitation with gigantic schemes of improvement. Overflowing streams of commerce circle the world. The human brain is under constant strain. Life has become strenuous. Everyone is throwing into the great cauldron of public opinion some scheme or plan or idea, practical or visionary, sensible or foolish, until it seems as though beside that cauldron were ever present the witches of Macbeth chanting:

"Double, double, toil and trouble;
Fire burn, and cauldron bubble."

Out of this tremendous activity, these gigantic combinations, will come achievements marvelous beyond even the flights of fancy. Into this century with all its possibilities you enter as young men. You have the grasp of a lifetime upon them. Your presence in this institution is to fit yourselves to take part in those achievements. I know not what may be your respective places in life.

The avenues of labor and usefulness are many and pointing in diverse directions. Business, science, art, medicine, law, theology—all are before you. In no country on the face of the globe is there an equal opportunity for the individual brain and the personal force. There is that freedom which gives ample scope for individual activities. All that you do and achieve will enter into and become part of the national glory or the national shame. You can make your names honored ones in the history of the republic, or by-words and a reproach. You may repeat the story of Alexander Hamilton, or that of Aaron Burr.

I cannot doubt your choice and purpose. No man covets infamy, and the young, thank God, have lofty ideals.

"Fear not to build thine eyrie in the heights
Where golden splendors play;
And trust thyself unto thine inmost soul,
In simple faith always;
For God will make divinely real
The highest forms of thine ideal."

How can those ideals be best incorporated into your lives and thus into the life of the nation? You know what a Christian home is, even if not brought up in one. Whether a humble one with scanty furnishings, or a more pretentious one with costlier adornments, in each you found truthfulness, purity; the spirit of peace was upon it; industry dwelt there, self-respect in the individual and mutual respect in all.

Will you add one more to the many of those homes in the land? You can bring to it strength and ability to work. You can bring culti-

"Will you add one more (Christian home) to the many of those homes in the land? ... Place the Bible on your table and enshrine the Master in your heart and you may be sure you are building up a home ... for the strength and glory of the republic." (Photo: Shutterstock)

vated intelligence and the delights of literature and science. You may introduce into it the sweet and refining touch of music and the other arts. You may place on the other side of the table the angel of the household, whose gentleness and grace add so much to the sweetness of home life.

Crown all these with the inspirations which come from Christianity, place the Bible on your table and enshrine the Master in your heart and you may be sure you are building up a home which will be not merely peace and blessing to you, but also for the strength and glory of the republic. And when the evening of life comes nigh and you see such homes multiply in the land, this nation become more thoroughly filled with the spirit and principles of Christianity, more justly and universally entitled to the appellation of a Christian nation, you will sing with Julia Ward Howe:

"Mine eyes have seen the glory of the coming of the Lord."

Afterword

One *Christian* Nation Under God

BY MARTIN MAWYER

J
ustice David Brewer may have been the first high-level government official to refer to America as a Christian nation—but he was not the last. In a letter to Pope Pius XII, President Harry S. Truman wrote, "Your Holiness, this is a Christian Nation." He went on to make a direct reference to Justice Brewer's ruling in the *Holy Trinity v. United States* court decision.

"More than a half century ago that declaration was written into the decrees of the highest court of this land," President Truman told the pontiff. "It is not without significance that the valiant pioneers who left Europe to establish settlements here, at the very beginning of their colonial enterprises, declared their faith in the Christian religion and made ample provision for its practice and for its support."

In 1931 the Supreme Court once again ruled, "We are a Christian people." The court made direct reference to Justice Brewer's 1892 decision for the basis of this claim.

The 1931 case involved a Canadian-born Baptist minister, Douglas Clyde Macintosh, who applied to become a naturalized U.S. citizen. Rev. Macintosh, though he previously served as a military chaplain for the Canadian Army during World War I, objected to swearing an oath of allegiance to the United States if it involved supporting a war that he found morally objectionable. As a result, the District Court of Connecticut denied Macintosh citizenship. An appellate court subsequently overturned the ruling, leading to the case arriving at the Supreme Court as *U.S. v. Macintosh*.

Writing for the majority in a 5-4 decision, Justice George Sutherland found that "We are a Christian people" and, as such, our obedience to the laws of the land is "not inconsistent with the will of God." In essence, the court determined that there is nothing in Christianity that would prevent citizens from following laws passed by a Christian people. This assumes, of course, that those who pass such laws have a basic understanding of the Bible and would never make an unchristian law, or cause its citizens to go into an unjust war.

This is not only a highly debatable opinion, but it sheds light on the whole matter of whether America wants to call itself a Christian nation, a secular nation, an atheist nation or some other type of hyphenated nation.

It's easy to understand that laws come from individuals who have enough collective votes to agree on the necessity of the law being passed. But what makes them agree? In 1931, the Supreme Court held that as "a Christian people," Americans make laws from a Christian perspective that would never collide with "the will of God."

That's not true today, of course. America is becoming mired in laws and policies that may rightfully be considered in direct conflict with "the will of God" from a Christian perspective. Delving into all these specific laws is not necessary to this discussion, but most are familiar with such conflicts as Christian bakers being forced to make wedding cakes in celebration of homosexual marriage, Christian resort owners being forced to host gay weddings, Christian evangelists being arrested for street preaching or Christian homeowners being fined for hosting Bible studies.

The point of the 1931 Supreme Court ruling is that laws come from a set of core beliefs. In the case of *United States v. Macintosh* it was understood that these beliefs originated in Christianity.

In contemporary America, this is no longer true. Even if we rightfully *still* call ourselves a Christian nation (meaning the vast majority of Americans consider themselves Christians), this no longer means the laws being passed are rooted in Christian ethics, morality or principles.

Starting in the late 20th century and now continuing into the 21st century, it has become publicly reprehensible and unacceptable to claim a law is being passed because it has roots in the Bible. It is universally understood in America that that if a law is being drafted, supported or promoted it must come from a nonsectarian point of view, meaning a secular perspective.

Secularism is defined as the separation of government from religion. Those promoting this viewpoint constantly use the phrase "separation of church and state" to add legal authority to their position. The phrase has been so often used that many (if not most) Americans believe it is written in the U.S. Constitution, which it is not.

Justice George Sutherland, front row, right, reaffirmed in a 1931 Supreme Court decision that "We are a Christian people." Our obedience to the laws of the land, therefore, is "not inconsistent with the will of God."

Thomas Jefferson is the original author of the phrase. In a letter to the Danbury Baptist Association in 1802, Jefferson said he felt the First Amendment to the Constitution built "a wall of separation between Church and State." The U.S. Supreme Court first used the phrase in 1878 in the case *Reynolds v. United States*. For nearly a century and a half afterwards, secularists have been employing the phrase to strip America of any type of religious symbol, activity, law or celebration in the public sphere.

There is no need to slog through the volumes of victories the secularists have achieved in eliminating religion (in particular, the Christian religion) from public view—religious monuments have been destroyed; public prayer has been banned; religious words have been censored; entire laws have been overturned; religious symbols have been removed, and, in some extreme cases, religious speech has been silenced.

It should probably be noted at this point that even if we accept that the words appearing in a letter from Thomas Jefferson should somehow carry the weight of law, Jefferson never said he wanted to build a "wall of separation between *Religion* and State." Instead, he advocated for a wall separating *Church* and State. His meaning is obvious. He did not want an organized church working hand in glove with government officials. It's preposterous, disingenuous and fanciful to think or expect government officials will not lean on their religious beliefs, however, in their support or opposition to policies, laws, ordinances, regulations or goals for America.

If this were not the case, the only suitable citizens that could be recruited for government would be atheists or people who are able to deny or set aside their faith while holding government office. Who would want such people running government? An atheist is nothing but a fool (Psalm 14:1). And a person who denies his faith is a hypocrite (1 Tim 4:2). If Thomas Jefferson meant to build a wall between *Religion* and State, we would have nothing but fools and hypocrites running government. (An appropriate *wink* should probably be inserted here.)

Unfortunately, it has now become normal and customary to accept the view that there should be a wall between *Religion* and Government in America, and that religious belief should not be a consideration when making government policies or laws.

This is a falsehood that even many Christians have grown to accept, either unashamedly or passively.

As an activist, I have been in the Christian advocacy movement for more than 30 years. I have had the great pleasure of meeting many Christian activists during those three decades. But it is not surprising that many of them avoid using the word "Christian" in their organizations' names: Family Research Council, Traditional Values Coalition, American Family Association, Concerned Women for America and Liberty Counsel, to name but a few. They correctly understand that as soon as they use the word "Christian" in their groups' names, the media will stop calling them, lawmakers will avoid them and policy makers will dismiss them as zealots trying to impose their religious views on America.

But ... is imposing religious views on America always a bad thing? The mere idea of it makes many cringe. Yet it is done all the time, mostly without fanfare or objection. Thou shalt not murder, bear false witness or steal are great examples of religious ideals being forced upon Americans without objection.

Many other decidedly Christian morals and laws are either imposed on American society or universally promoted as honorable behavior. There are laws against rape, incest, usury, assault and battery, extortion, fraud, slander and kidnapping that Americans must obey, and which are also found in the Bible. America also promotes such biblical virtues as honesty, marital fidelity, honoring parents, responsible parenting and obeying government authorities. America also frowns on such biblical misbehavior as cheating, coveting, violence, greed and corruption.

These are not humanist values, as some would like us to believe. These values and laws existed long before the philosophy of "humanism" (a method of critical thinking of dubious origin, though no earlier than the 15th century) even existed. These are values and laws of decidedly Judeo-Christian origin. Nowhere in America is anyone claiming that they unduly impose religion on someone else.

Christian-inspired laws, morals, ethics and principles ARE American. This is exactly why the Supreme Court in 1931 declared, "We are a Christian people" and that following such laws "is not inconsistent with the will of God."

Americans should have little or no fear of legislators passing laws based on their Christian beliefs. All they need to do is look at the centuries of American laws that have already been enacted and are derived from Christian concepts. They can take further comfort in the fact that virtually all Christian laws follow the standard set forth by Jesus Christ: "Love they neighbor as thyself."

Murder does not constitute this love. Nor do rape, theft, bearing false witness and so forth.

If Americans should have any fear of religious values being imposed on the nation through lawmaking, it should be directed at the secular humanists whose dictates are not only pious and morally superior, but often oppressive and absurd. Examples of these arbitrary laws include the banning of large-sized soft drinks (New York City), the outlawing of McDonald's Happy Meals (San Francisco), traffic tickets for having a muddy vehicle (Minnesota), making it a crime to collect rainwater on your own property (Utah) and handing out citations to car owners with trash in their vehicles (Hilton Head, S.C.). There are far too many of these man-made crazy laws to enumerate here.

The point is that all laws come from someone's personal or religious beliefs. An individual's claim that his law is based on personal belief—rather than religious belief—does not automatically elevate that law and make it acceptable, reasonable or credible. In fact, man-made, personal laws are threatening to turn our law-enforcement officers into the Super Nanny Police. Rather than fighting real crime, police officers are on the lookout for people smoking in public parks, kids selling lemonade on street corners, or (in New York) people taking photos of themselves with lions, tigers or other big cats. In California, law enforcement must be on the lookout for men and women who have sex with each other without first making "an affirmative, conscious and voluntary agreement to engage in sexual activity"!

Christian laws are not oppressive and intrusive, but secular humanist laws are often the definition of despotism and repression. In Atlanta, a fire chief was fired in 2016 simply for writing a Christian-oriented book. That's oppression, domination and persecution—the very things secular humanists claim to fear about Christian-based laws.

It is not Christians, but rather the secularists who are determined to impose their values on the nation under threat of fines, jail time or loss of employment.

The truth is, America *is* a Christian nation.

According to a 2015 Pew Research Center survey, the Muslim population in America is one percent. Hindus account for only .07 percent. Jews were only slightly ahead of both minorities at a meager 1.8 percent. The Buddhist population wasn't even large enough for the Pew Research Center to sample.

Christians, however, represent 75 percent of Americans. And, of those Americans who claim any sort of religious belief, 94 percent identify as Christian.

The Pew Research Center is unabashed in saying, "America remains a predominantly Christian nation." Since "predominant" means "present as the strongest element, exertion or power," the strongest element in America, according to the Pew Research Center, is Christians.

More Americans read the Bible than any other book ever published. No other book in the United States resides in more American homes than does the Bible, with 88 percent of households owning at least one copy. Most Americans own multiple copies, on average 4.4.

To tell a Bible-believing nation that it must dispense with its faith when passing laws, ordinances, policies and regulations is nothing short of denying these people citizenship. America is not a nation of secularists and atheists. Why should the philosophy of God-deniers be the only privileged class to make American laws? Why should Christians be forced to deny that their faith has any bearing on the laws they support, propose or pass?

But the mind-set seems to be well established in America that laws should not come from a religious conscience. When is the last time anyone in America heard of a legislator offering a law because of his or her Christian beliefs?

We are a Christian nation because the people in America are decidedly Christian. Still, our laws, institutions and policies are quickly becoming unchristian, mainly because Christians have been committing political suicide for nearly a century. Blame it on Supreme Court rulings, media bashings, secular education or weak churches; Christians in America routinely censor themselves out of fear of violating some fictitious "separation of Church and State" standard.

Christians are denying their own citizenship, goaded by a secular, liberal and hedonistic society that wants to put their faith in chains and muzzle their mouths.

The brilliance of Justice Brewer's book, *The United States: A Christian Nation,* is that it speaks to the duty that Christians owe their nation and their fellow Americans—*because of their Christian faith and beliefs.*

What has Christianity done for America?

Justice Brewer provides the answers.

"It has stood for liberty and the rights of man," Justice Brewer writes. "And the more thoroughly this republic is filled with the spirit of the Gospel, the more universal the rule of Christianity in the hearts of our people, the more certainly will she ever be the welcome leader in movements for peace among the nations."

As Christians we should neither be embarrassed nor cowardly in projecting our faith into the laws of the nation. Christian laws and principles are the foundational concrete upon which the American justice system and guiding doctrines were founded.

These timeless words by Justice Brewer should be taught, revered and emblazoned upon the American consciousness:

"I could show how largely our laws and customs are based upon the laws of Moses and the teachings of Christ; how constantly the Bible is appealed to as the guide of life and the authority in questions of morals; how Christian doctrines are accepted as the great comfort in times of sorrow and affliction, and fill with the light of hope the services for the dead. On every hilltop towers the steeple of some Christian church, while from the marble witnesses in God's acre comes the universal but silent testimony to the common faith in the Christian doctrine of the resurrection and the life hereafter.

"Christianity was a primary cause of the first settlement on our shores; that the organic instruments, charters and constitutions of the colonies were filled with abundant recognitions of it as a controlling factor in the life of the people; that in one of them, at least, it was in terms declared the established religion, while in several the furthering of Christianity was stated to be one of the purposes of the govern; in many faith in it was a condition of holding office; in some, authority was given to the legislature to make its support a public charge; in nearly all the constitutions there has been an express recognition of the sanctity of the Christian Sunday; the God of the Bible is appealed to again and again.

"And so I might go on with illustration after illustration showing how the faith of the Christian has stood in times of trial and trouble as the rock upon which the nation has rested.

"I insist that Christianity has been so wrought into the history of this republic, so identified with its growth and prosperity, has been and is so dear to the hearts of the great body of our citizens, that it ought not to be spoken of contemptuously or treated with ridicule."

Whether the United States is a Christian nation matters only if Christians have dominance in America—over its government, social institutions, media, education, social networks, businesses, entertainment, policies, goals and justice system. If Christians are merely spectators, their overwhelming numbers do not matter. They will be merely spectators at a football game, outnumbering the players but unable to make the rules or determine an outcome that will affect not only the teams, but the spectators as well.

Christians must ask themselves: Why should we allow the unbelieving, the Jesus-haters, those who mock Christianity — to rule over our lives? They cannot, unless we allow them to. We still have the ball. We have the numbers. But we need to rise up from our seats and perform our Christian duty to America.

About the Author

Christian Action Network (CAN) was founded in 1990 by Martin Mawyer. Based in Lynchburg, Virginia, the group is a public advocacy and education organization based on biblical principles, values, traditions and American ideals. Its primary goals are to protect America's religious and moral heritage through educational efforts.

Prior to founding Christian Action Network, Mawyer was Editor-in-Chief of the Rev. Jerry Falwell's Moral Majority Report, and author of **Silent Shame: The Alarming Rise of Child Sexual Abuse**. In 1990 Mawyer formed his own public advocacy group, often continuing to work with Falwell on joint projects and public campaigns.

He has since authored three additional books, including his latest work: **Twilight in America: The Untold Story of Islamic Terrorist Training Camps Inside America.**

CAN accomplishes its education work through direct-mail campaigns aimed at impacting public policy, along with public speaking engagements, documentary films, radio and TV interviews, books, and alliances with other organizations to impact change.

Under Mawyer's leadership, CAN has grown to more than 150,000 members. In addition to writing four books, he has directed three documentary films and has appeared on the top television and radio programs in the country, including *Larry King Live, The O'Reilly Factor, The Hannity Show, NBC's Today Show, Pat Robertson's 700 Club,* and *Entertainment Tonight.*

Mawyer has been married for 40 years to his wife, Bonnie. Together they have four children and four grandchildren.

33375095R00045

Made in the USA
Middletown, DE
11 July 2016